KNOSSOS

THE PALACE OF MINOS

A SURVEY OF THE MINOAN CIVILIZATION
AND
A GUIDE TO THE MUSEUM OF HERAKLION

Mythology - Archaeology - History - Museum -
Excavations-Explanatory text of map.

SUPERVISION OF TEXTS: MRS. SOSSO LOGIADOU - PLATONOS
ARCHAEOLOGIST

ATHENS

COPYRIGHT **CHR. Z. MATHIOULÁKIS** PUBLISHER

ISBN 960-7310-46-2

«Κρήτη τις γαῖ' ἔστι, μέσῳ ἐνὶ οἴνοπι πόντῳ,
καλὴ καὶ πίειρα, περίρρυτος· ἐν δ' ἄνθρωποι
πολλοί, ἀπειρέσιοι, καὶ ἐννήκοντα πόληες
ἄλλη δ' ἄλλων γλῶσσα μεμιγμένη· ἐν μὲν Ἀχαιοὶ
ἐν δ' Ἐτεόκρητες μεγαλήτορες, ἐν δὲ Κύδωνες,
Δωριέες τε τριχάϊκες δῖοί τε Πελασγοὶ
τῇσι δ' ἐνὶ Κνωσός, μεγάλη πόλις· ἔνθα τε Μίνως
ἐννέωρος βασίλευε· Διὸς μεγάλου ὀαριστής,
πατρὸς ἐμοῖο πατήρ, μεγαλοθύμου Δευκαλίωνος,
Δευκαλίων δ' ἐμὲ τίκτε καὶ Ἰδομενῆα ἄνακτα...»

(HOMER ODYSSÈE τ. 172-180)

2

KNOSSOS

HISTORICAL INTRODUCTION

Archaeological excavation to date has established that Crete was first inhabited during the Neolithic period, about 6000-5000 B.C. The men of that time were farmers, knew how to work stone, and used clay for the first time to make pots. They were scattered throughout the entire island and dwelt mainly in caves, as at Zakro and Ayia Fotia in Eastern Crete, at Amnisos in the mountains of Lassithi in Central Crete and at Yerakari near Rethymno , Koumarospilo, Platyvola and Gavdos in the West. At the same time, however, they began to build settlements, remains of which have been found in the lowest levels at Knossos and Phaistos, and isolated houses, such as those at Katsambas (Heraklion) and Magassa (Sitia).

About 2600 B.C. there was a migration of peoples from Asia Minor, and perhaps also from Libya, and the island saw the beginning of the famous M i n o a n C i v i l i s a t i o n. This is divided into four chronological periods, based on the initial construction, the destruction, the reconstruction and the final destruction of the palace-centers on the island.
1. Prepalatial (2600-1900 B.C.)
2. Protopalatial (1900-1700 B.C.)
3. Neopalatial (1700-1380 B.C.)
4. Postpalatial (1380-1100 B.C.)

The most important palaces were discovered in Central and Eastern Crete (Knossos, Phaistos, Malia and Zakro), though in the west, too, archaeology has recently begun to bring to light the ruins of a notable centre within the city of Khania.

First place amongst the palaces is held by that of Minos — the mythical king whose name was applied by Evans to the Minoan civilisation — at Knossos. Its life commenced about 1900 B.C., at the beginning of the Protopalatial period. At this point, for some unknown reason, a number of royal families over the whole island acquired supreme power and began to build palaces. The one at Knossos was built on a low hill ("Kefala") and covered an area of 22,000 square metres. The city of Knossos, the importance of which may be estimated from its two harbours, was built around it. One of the harbours was at K a t s a m b a s, near the mouth of the river Kairatos, which flows to the south and east of the hill of Knossos. The other, A m n i s s o s, to the east of Heraklion, was referred to by Homer as the second harbour of Knossos. The two harbours presuppose the existence of a large city. According to Evans it had a population of 80,000, though more recent scholars put the figure at 30,000 (Faure). "Minos" may have been the title of the king of Knossos, in much the same way as the Egyptian kings were called "Pharaohs".

The first palace at Knossos was destroyed in 1700 B.C., probably by an earthqake. A brilliant new building was immediately built in its place. This in turn was destroyed by earthquake in 1450, and re-built when the Achaeans of mainland Greece settled on the island. The palace was thus under Achaean domination in its final phase. It suffered its final destruction at the beginning of the 14th century. Some parts of it were inhabited by refugees until 1100 B.C., when the Dorians reached Crete and put an end to the Minoan civilisation, which was now in decline. It was replaced by the purely Greek civilisation of the Geometric period.

After the final destruction of the palace, the ruins of it were covered with earth as time went by, so that nothing could be seen of this enormous multi-storey group of buildings, with their approximately 1500 rooms, until the excavations of Evans. Its reminiscense, however, was preserved in the traditions and the myths of the Greeks, as the Labyrinth; that is, a huge building with many winding corridors, from which it was difficult to find a way out. The true meaning of the Labyrinth emerged after the excavation of the palace and the discovery of the Cretan civilisation. It derives from the word l a b r y s, meaning double axe, which is thought to have been the most sacred symbol of Minoan religion. The "Labyrinth" was thus the palace itself, the "House of the Double Axes", and the main sanctuary of the deity.

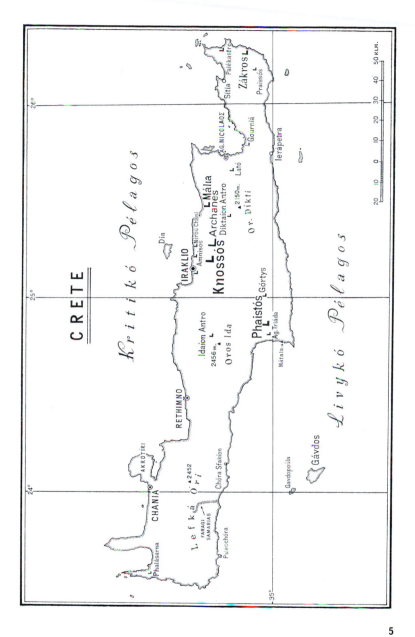

CRETE

Kritikó Pélagos

Livykó Pélagos

Phalásarna
AKROTÍRI
CHANIÁ
Lefká Óri ▲2452
FARAGI SAMARIÁS
Chóra Sfakíon
Paleochóra

RETHIMNO

Idaion Antro 2456 m. ▲
Oros Ida

Gavdopoúla
Gávdos

Mátala
Phaistós L Ag.Triáda
L Górtys
Knossós L
Archánes L
Níroù Cháni L
Amnisós L
IRAKLIO L
Día
L Mália
Diktaíon Antro L
▲2150 m.
Or. Dikti

AG.NICOLAOΣ
L Gourniá
Latό L
Ierápetra L

Sitía
Zákros L
Praissós L
Palékastro
Zákros

50 KLM.
40 30 20 10 0 10 20

24° 25° 26°
35°

Sir Arthur Evans

HISTORY OF THE EXCAVATIONS

AT KNOSSOS

It had long been known that there had once existed a city called Knossos in this region, and indeed, the inhabitants often found ancient objects as they cultivated their fields.

The first man to excavate in the area was Minos Kalokairinos, a merchant of Heraklion, and a lover of antiquity. In 1878 he uncovered two of the palace store-rooms. The Turkish owners of the land compelled him to stop his investigations, and the attempts of Schliemann to purchase the "Kefala" hill came to nought because of the excessive sums they demanded. Fortune thus played a part in assisting Arthur Evans to begin systematic excavation in 1900, when the island had now been declared an independent State. He was at that time Director of the Ashmolean Museum in Oxford, and first visited Crete in order to study and decipher the unknown script that could be made out on sealstones.

The excavations began at a very rapid pace, and by the end of 1903 almost all of the palace had been uncovered and work began on the surrounding area. Evans continued his researches until 1931, with an interruption for the duration of the First World War. He subsequently published his work in four volumes entitled "The Palace of Minos at Knossos". His chief assistant was the archaeologist D. Mackenzie, who kept the basic day-book of the excavations.

From the beginning it proved necessary to preserve and restore the monuments that were being uncovered. A number of parts of the palace were restored in this way, and considerable use was made of reinforced cement in the work. The parts of the restoration that represent timber frames and other wooden structures were formerly painted yellow (the yellow colour has now been replaced by a colour conventionally representing the wood). In a number of places, moreover, copies were installed of the marvellous frescoes discovered during the excavation of the palace. This method of restoration has received much criticism, since it used materials foreign to Minoan architecture. Some scholars also dispute some of the conclusions of the pioneer English excavator.

All these questions aside, E v a n s is constantly admired for his intuition, his creative imagination and his profound scholarship. It is basically to him that we owe the discovery of the marvellous Minoan world, which until his time was only dimly reflected in Greek mythology. His services have brought him international fame and recognition.

As a mark of honour, therefore, and to perpetuate his memory, his bust has been erected on the south side of the west court of the palace.

After his death responsibility for the excavations at Knossos, which continue to the present day, was assumed by the British School of Archaeology.

TOUR AT THE PALACE OF KNOSSOS

(See map).

The palace was the residence and headquarters of the king, the office-bearers and the priests, and although it was an administrative and economic centre, it also had a sacred character.

The palace is divided into two wings by the Central Court: the West wing **A** which housed the religious and official state rooms, and the East wing **B** where the domestic quarter and workshops were to be found.

WEST WING A

We enter the palace from the western approach, **A,** which is in the form of a ramp, and come first to the **paved west court I.** This is crossed by passages of slightly raised paved slabs, which are known as **processional ways,** because it is believed that the religious processions passed along them during the sacred ceremonies. One passage leads NE to the "Theatre", and a second to the South, to the palace.

In the West court there are **two altars 2** and three very large circular walled pits ('Kouloures'), which had been filled with the broken pottery used in the sacred rites **3.** At the bottom of the west and central pits, remains were found of houses dating from the end of the Prepalatial period. Houses of the Neopalatial period were excavated to the North of the pits, and tubular vases that had a religious function (the sacred snakes were kept in them) were discovered there. These may be seen in Heraklion Museum (room IV, case 46).

On the eastern side of the court rises the west façade of the palace, the lower courses of which consist of large gypsum blocks, blackened by the fire that destroyed the palace.

We enter the palace through the **West Porch 4,** a structure supported by a central column. Part of the base of this column, made of gypsum, survives in a good state of preservation (Minoan columns were made of wood, tapered from top to bottom, and stood on stone bases). The east wall of the Porch was decorated with a large fresco depicting a bullfight (only a part of the bull's foot is preserved). Two rooms open to the South of this area: the small one served as a **Gate-keeper's lodge 5,**while the larger of the two, **6,** which may have held a throne, was used by the king to follow the rituals in the West court.

We now follow the **Corridor of the Procession 7,** which takes its name from the large fresco discovered here, depicting young men and women, almost life-size, bringing gifts to a female figure, who will have been a queen or a goddess. This corridor gives a good idea of the grandeur and luxury of the Minoan palaces: walls covered with multi-coloured frescoes, and a floor of white gypsum slabs, combined with smaller slabs of green schist, with red stucco in the joints between them. The corridor today comes to an abrupt end. In its original form it continued for about ten more paces to the SW corner (where the SW entrance was), turned left and ran along the whole length of the South side of the palace. At this point there was a terraced-portico. Underneath the corridor and the portico there were semi-basement rooms which are in a good state of preservation.

As we cannot today follow the Corridor of the Procession in order to enter the palace, we use the double door in the corner to our left, behind the large red column (restored area).

The small building that can be seen to the right, on a lower level, is the **South House 8.** It was built during the penultimate building phase, and may have belonged to the high priest of the palace.

The Corridor of the Procession had two passages leading to the main palace. One **9** is to the South and leads to the **Central Court 10.** The other takes one through the **South Propylaeum 11** to the first floor of the west wing of the palace. The SW part of the Propylaeum was restored by Evans. The walls were covered with frescoes, which probably formed a continuation of the procession fresco, except that whereas the latter portrayed young women as well as men, this one has only young men. (In Minoan frescoes, the bodies of men are indicated by a satiated red colour and those of women by white. Men and women both have long hair and wear similar clothes and jewellery - bracelets on the arms, anklets on the legs and a sealstone on the wrist). The best preserved of the figures is the famous "Cupbearer", so called after the conical libation vase (rhyton) that he is holding. This youth typifies the ideal male figure of the period, with his slender waist, emphasized by the decorative metal belt. He is wearing a kilt which ends in a network, held in position by small weights of lead.

In the NE part of the Propylaeum can be seen a number of jars that were in fragments when they were discovered here and have since been reconstituted. They were undoubtedly placed here during the period of the "re-occupation" of the palace, when the Propylaeum was used as a store room.

To the North of the South Propylaeum there is a broad open **staircase 12** leading to the first floor, where the official rooms of the sanctuary **(piano nobile) 13** were located. From the top of the staircase there is a complete view of the surrounding area, with its row of hills, luxurious vegetation and the river Kairatos. Below, and slightly to the left, at the level of the Corridor of the Procession, we can distinguish the sacred horns; according to one theory they originally stood on the south side of the palace roof.

The staircase flanked by colonnaded porticoes, the bases of which are the only parts preserved, leads to the entrance of the Sanctuary. Immediately after this there is an anteroom and a room identified by Evans as the **Tri-columnar Shrine 14,**depicted in frescoes. Of the shrine's three columns and three pillars, only a few of the bases are preserved. In the middle of this floor there was a corridor running the whole length of it; this corridor was parallel to the one on the ground floor that runs the length of the store rooms and can be seen below and to the West. These store-rooms are known as the **"West Magazines" 15,** and there were originally twenty-one of them; three of them fell into disuse during the Protopalatial period, however, and there are therefore only eighteen surviving today. There are magazines in other parts of the palace, too, and the visitor may justifiably ask himself why there were so many storage areas. We must not forget that the king of Knossos, was a supreme secular and religious ruler. The magazines were therefore necessary in order to store the offerings to the deity, the taxes, the gifts and the revenue of the kingdom. The pithoi that can be seen today were used to hold oil and wine, and possibly also cereals, though few remains of the last have been found. The stone cists ("kaselles") in front of the pithoi may have contained precious vessels and vases; some of them certainly contained tools and weapons, as may be deduced from references in the tablets found here. There were other kaselles, finally, built below the floor of the **Corridor of the Magazines 16;** they were lined with sheets of lead, and were used to store liquids, or in some cases served as repositories. The west complex of the magazines, as Evans thinks, was contemporary with the first palace,

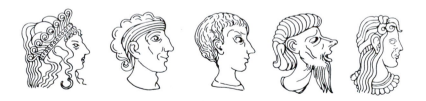

Minoan Types

from the 19th century, though it was also reused later, after the 17th century reconstruction. The magazines and corridor had neither windows nor light-wells, but were illuminated by oil lamps. The oil in the stores caught fire during the final destruction of the palace, and this caused the blackening on the walls. The stone pyramid-shaped bases that can be seen in the corridor were used to support large double axes.

Returning to the room of the "Tricolumnar Shrine", we come to the so called **"Great Hall" 17,** to the West of it, which has two columns in the middle of it. Two thirds of this room have been restored. It is, in fact, a particularly impressive area. Almost nothing has survived of the upper stories, either at Knossos or at the other Minoan palace structures, since, with the exception of the Grand Staircase on the east side, they were constructed of materials incapable of withstanding the frequent earthquakes.

From the northern edge of this floor we can see the difference in the thickness of the walls down on the ground floor. The first and the third are quite thin, while the second and fourth are thicker. This difference results directly from the need to support the colonnades of the upper quarters. To the North of the 'Great Hall' is the so called **"Room of the Sanctuary" 18,** which has six columns.

We proceed to the right to the **rooms 19** which have been restored on the basis of the plan of the ground floor walls. Copies of frescoes discovered at various points of the palace and now in the Heraklion Museum are displayed here. They fall into two groups, the purely decorative, with geometric compositions, and those depicting scenes from daily life, cult scenes and sacred rituals of the Minoans.

The east wall has the Toreador fresco. This was a contest or game involving young men and girls and a bull. It required exceptional dexterity and daring (they grasped the horns of the bull, executed a double somersault on its back and lept to the ground on the other side) and frequently became dangerous. This contest, which was a particular favourite of the Minoans, should in no way be identified with the modern bull-fight, in which the aim is to overcome and kill the bull. Since the bull was a sacred animal, the contest might even be thought of as a ritual act,forming part of the total structure of religion. The fresco was discovered in the east wing of the palace.

To the left, on the north wall, may be seen the fresco of the 'Ladies in Blue', one of the first examples of Minoan painting. This was also discovered in the east wing.

To the left again, on the west wall, are displayed the two miniature frescoes, which were discovered in the throne room. Both of them depict festivals in the palace, in what one might call an impressionistic manner. The lower has a picture of women dancing in the sacred grove of Knossos. The spectators following it are the men on red. They are all greatly enjoying the spectacle and are raising their hands in applause. The upper fresco has a scene of a religious gathering in an outdoor area of the palace; this may be the central court, with the façade of the Columnar shrine in the centre. There are two more frescoes beyond and to the left of the door, and a third exhibited opposite. All three were found in the "House of the Frescoes", and depict exotic gardens, with flowers and plants in a variety of colours, a blue bird and two blue monkeys. It is clear that the monkeys are tame from the ribbon around their heads and from their ability to carry out some task (in one fresco they are gathering papyrus reeds, and in the other plants that look like papyrus).

Finally, the small fresco of the Minoan officer leading black mercenaries also comes from the "House of the Frescoes".

We descend a spiral staircase, to the North of the rooms we are in, to the **Anteroom 20** of the Throne room on the ground floor. In the centre of this room, which opens into the Central Court, there is a porphyry bassin which Evans thought was used for ritual lustration (it was discovered nearby). There are stone benches to the right and left, and, during the excavations, carbonised remains of a wooden seat were discovered in the space between them on the north side; a wooden throne a copy of that in the next room has therefore been placed here . The Anteroom leads into the **"Throne Room" 21,** which name derives from the small gypsum throne that was preserved intact in the position it still occupies today[1] as were the stone benches. The room very probably had a religious function, the priest-king sitting on the throne, with the priests on either side on the benches. The sacred nature of the area is also idicated by the lustral basin opposite (this is clearly not a bath, since it has no drain). The purification ritual will have been symbolic: those involved descended the small flight of steps, thus coming closer to mother earth, and there were their bodies sprinkled with holy water. A photograph is particularly important, since it shows a number of loaf-shaped alabaster vases on the floor, and a broken pithos in the corner. It is thought that at the time the palace was destroyed, a ritual was taking place in this area to appease the divinities, and that it was abruptly broken off, so that these vessels were left in position.

The north and west walls of the room were decorated with a large fresco representing griffins amongst reed-like vegetation, that may be seen in the restored copies. The griffin is thought to have symbolised the three forms of the deity: the heavenly, with its eagle's head, the earthly, with its lion's body, and the subterranean, with its tail in the form of a snake.

---

[1] The President of the International Court at the Hague has a seat that is a copy of this throne, since the Minos was thought to be the first judge in the world.

Further inside this room there was a small **niche 22** on a podium. According to Evans the priest-king withdrew into the inner area to fast and meditate. The area, which was dark, was lit by a stone lamp.

We emerge onto the **Central Court,** one of the most characteristic features of Minoan palace architecture. The different parts of the palace were built around it, and it is probable that ritual ceremonies were held here, so that a large audience could follow them. In the corner of the court we can see, as we come out of the Throne room, part of the drainage system. Stone drains lead the rain water to a central sewer.

The Central Court was paved, but very few traces of the paving have been preserved. Proceeding South from the Throne room, we come to the **Central Staircase 23,** of which only four steps are preserved today. It originally had two flights, and on the lower, broader one, there were large columns supporting the roof, the bases of which can still be seen amidst the steps.

To the left, next to the Central Staircase, is the façade of the **Tripartite Shrine** 24. Traces of the circular column bases can be made out on the stylobate. The middle was higher than the rest, and supported a central column. There were sacred horns between the columns and on the entablature. To the South, there are some steps leading to an anteroom with a stone seat, where the traces of the fire that finally destroyed the palace can clearly be distinguished. We now move on to the **Shrine of the Pillar Crypts 25.** The first room, to the right of the anteroom is known as "**The Room of the Tall Pithos**" **26.** Here we see one of the finest pithoi from the first neopalatial phase; it was discovered intact and remains **in situ.** Next door, to the left, are the "**Temple Repositories**" **27.** These two large storage-chests, built below the floor, were made of poros stone and were provided with sheets of lead, against damp. In them were found the most famous of the Minoan figurines, the "Snake Goddesses". The chests were covered in at a later date and three smaller ones built on top of them.

To the west of the Ante-room of the Crypts are the **Square-Pillar Crypts 28.** The Double Axe has been incised a large number of times on each pillar. There are rectangular stone basins near each column, for offerings of animal sacrifices. One of the rooms to the right was used as a store-room, and in the other is preserved a low ledge with vats. To the South of the ante-room is the area of the **Chariot tablets 29,** and still further to the South, an area occupied by a temple of Greek times (Temple of Rhea) **30;** in the room contiguous with it there is a clay bath tub, in which Linear B tablets were found.

We now return to the Central Court. The end of the Corridor of the Procession may be seen on the south side. As we have seen, this corridor ran the whole length of the south side of the palace, turned left again, and came out onto the Central Court.

The remains of one of the most famous frescoes, the **Priest-king, or Prince with the Lilies 31** were found in pieces on the floor somewhere in this area.

The youth, in low relief, is wearing a crown of lilies and peacock feathers, a gold necklace with beads in the form of lilies, and a simple kilt, secured by a broad belt. He may have been leading the sacred griffin or a sphinx on a rope. The scene is greatly restored, very few pieces of the original being preserved (part of the feathers of the crest, the chest, the two legs and the arm of the prince).

Below, in the middle of the south side of the palace was the **South Entrance B.**

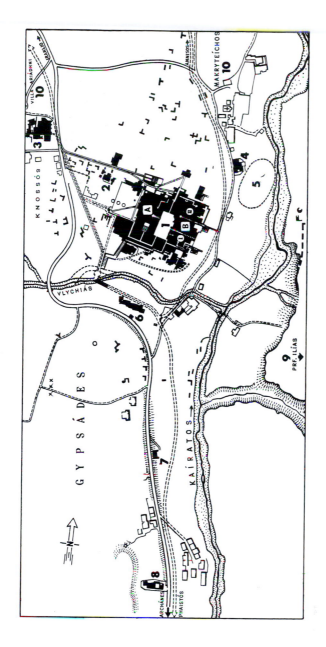

1. The Palace of Knossos. 2. The House of the Frescoes. 3. The Little Palace. 4. The Royal Villa. 5. The Arena. 6. The Guest-House (Caravanserai). 7. The House of the High Priest. 8. The Royal Temple Tomb. 9. The Minoan Cemeteries. 10. Roman Antiquities.

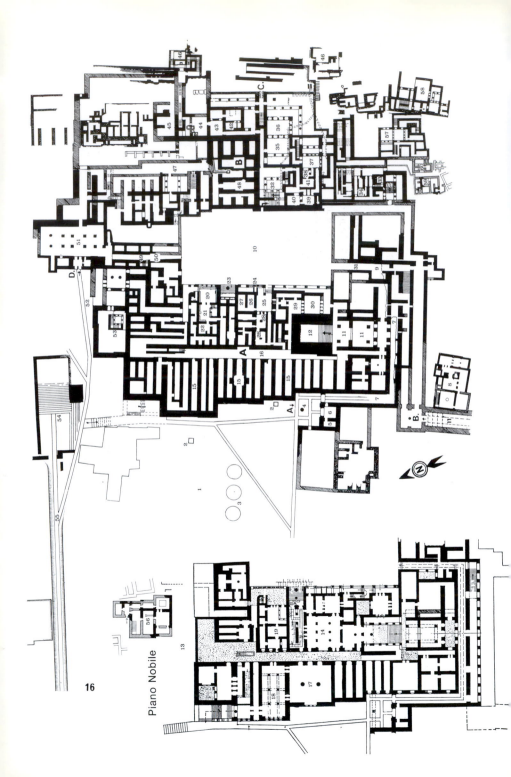

16

Piano Nobile

LEGEND

A. West Entrance.
B. South Entrance.
C. East Entrance.
D. North Entrance.

A West Wing.

1. West Court.
2. Altars.
3. Sacred Waste Pits, ('Koulouras').
4. West Porch.
5. Gate-keeper's Lodge.
6. Room with Throne.
7. Corridor of the Procession.
8. South House.
9. Corridor to the Central Court.
10. Central Court.
11. South Propylaeum.
12. Staircase.
13. Piano Nobile.
14. Tri-Columnar Shrine.
15. West Magazines.
16. Corridor of the Magazines.
17. Great Hall.
18. Room of the Shrine.
19. Rooms with copies of frescoes.
20. Anteroom to the Throne Room.
21. Throne Room.
22. Interior Shrine.
23. Central Staircase.
24. Tri-partite Shrine.
25. Anteroom of the Pillar Crypts.
26. Room of the Tall Pithos.
27. Temple Repositories.
28. Pillar Crypts.
29. Area of the "Chariot Tablets".
30. "Temple of Rhea".
31. The Prince with the Lilies.
32. Grand Staircase.
33. Shrine of the Double Axes.
34. Lustral Basin.
35. Hall of the Double Axes or
36. King's Megaron.
37. Queen's Megaron.
38. Queen's Bathroom.

B East Wing.

39. Queen's Toilet Room.
40. Court of the Distaffs.
41. Treasury.
42. Lapidary's Workshop.
43. Potter's Workshop.
44. Court of the Stone Spout.
45. Magazines of the Giant Pithoi.
46. East Bastion.
47. Corridor of the Draught Board.
48. Magazine of the Pithoi with Medallions.
49. Bastion of the N. Entrance.
50. Passage of the N. Entrance.
51. "Custom House".
52. NW Entrance.
53. Lustral Basin.
54. Theatre.
55. Royal Road.
56. House of the Frescoes.
57. House of the Chancel Screen.
58. SE House.
59. House of the Sacrified Oxen.
60. House of the Fallen Blocks.

EAST WING B

Whereas the West wing opposite had only two stories in addition to the ground floor on the level of the Central Court, the East wing had four stories as well as a ground floor. Communication between them was by the **Grand Staircase 32,** one of the best preserved parts of the palace. From the landing we can see the first floor, which has been restored, almost on a level with the Court. From this point to the ground floor, there are four surviving flights of stairs, the first two of which are restored, while the lower two are preserved just as they were found. There are also traces of a fifth flight. This staircase formed the official approach to the royal quarters, though there were also auxiliary staircases for daily use.

The walls of the landings of the staircase were covered with fresco paintings; a copy of one of these may be seen on the east wall of the adjoining verandah depicting shields on a frieze of spiral. There are no shields surviving from this period, for they were made of ox-hide (the shape of them is known from small specimens in ivory or other materials, and also from the descriptions in Homer's Iliad). In the Iliad they are described as "seven-oxhide shields" — that is of seven skins sewn one on top of the other.

We pass through a door in the south side of the landing, through a crooked corridor and some other apartments and come to a room with a bath. Amongst the pottery found hereby were a few vases decorated with white lilies. Further it can be seen part of the drainage system, with stone conduits. To the South of it is the **"Shrine of the Double Axes" 33,** which is today covered over.

Two pairs of sacred horns still stand on a pedestal on the north side, and next to them are clay figurines of a goddess and worshippers. The shrine belongs to the post-palace period. A short way to the South there is a **Lustral Basin 34,** similar to the one in the Throne room.

Returning to the landing with the shields, we descend the Grand Staircase to the ground floor. We now get a better view, from the small colonnade running alongside the area of the central light-well system that supplies light vertically to all the floors. A system of light-wells was generally used in the residential quarters of all the Minoan palaces. It supplies light and air indirectly to each successive floor, and mitigates the summer heat, while also protecting the rooms from the cold of winter.

The gypsum slabs of the colonnades and of the East-West corridor adjoining it, are in a very good state of preservation. At the beginning of the corridor there is a small doorway and it is possible to see how the door operated from the traces remaining on the threshold. The hinge and the rub marks show that the wooden door opened to the right.

From the corridor we enter the **Hall of the Double Axes 35,** or the **King's Megaron 36** to the right. The two sections of which it consists communicate with each other through a tier of doorways, which continues through to the colonnade of the light well in the east. The two light-wells at the sides of the room are based on a vertical system of natural ventilation, which achieves a regular circulation of air between them. At the ground level of the light well we can distinguish part of the circuit drainage system. The ashlar stones of the west light well have the sacred double axe which gave the room its name, incised on them in a number of places. The quarter towards the East light well was probably used for audiences with the king, for remains of a throne were found here. On the gypsum, which has been calcinated by fire, it is possible to make out traces of the canopy that covered the throne supported on columns.

The east section of the Hall is one of the grandest parts of the palace, with the triple tier of doorways that closed it in on three sides and with its external angular colonnade.

In Minoan times, large figure of eight shields of ox-hide hung on the north wall, where Evans placed a wooden throne.

Passing through a small door in the South of the Hall of the Double Axes, we proceed along a crooked corridor and come to the **Queen's Megaron 37,** a room smaller than that of the king, but equally imposing with its two light-wells. This room communicates with the east light well by means of two columns, the bases of which are in a good state of preservation today. Some parts of the floor have been removed, to reveal earlier paved surfaces, constructed at different periods and in different ways. The lowest is made of rough stones, the middle one of slabs in mosaic, and the uppermost of finely worked gypsum slabs. The fresco on the east wall, with the dolphins, fish and sea-urchins, belongs to neopalatial periods; during the last, it was covered by another with a frieze of spirals. Another fresco in this room, on a post of the east partition, shows a girl dancing, with her hair blowing in the wind as she turns. Her dress is particularly interesting, with its short-sleeved bolero, decorated with coloured embroidery (the original fresco is in Heraklion Museum).

To the west is the **Queen's Bathroom 38.** The bath, which was restored from fragments, is, like all the others, a small sitting bath. Both the walls of the small corridor through which we passed, and the lower parts of the walls of the bathroom were faced with tall gypsum slabs; the upper part of the walls was covered with monochrome frescoes, transversed by decorative friezes. The small wall painting here is the original, but the colours are not very well preserved. The column in the bathroom was restored in accordance with the traces preserved on the base of it. According to Evans, traces of three columns of the same style were found during the excavation of the Little Palace. They are reminiscent of Egyptian models, with capitals imitating lotus in blossoms.

Going through the small door in,the South of the bathroom and along the corridor beyond it, we come to the **Queen's Toilet Room 39.** The door and window of this room open on to a light well which is called the **Court of the Distaffs 40,** since the symbol of the distaff is incised on the wall. The low ledge along the south wall was used to hold the utensils for the toilet. Above this point there was a cistern and two conduits built into the wall, which carried the rainwater and the waste from the toilets on the floor above into the drains of the toilet next door, in the small room to the east. There is a groove in the partitions of this room, on the right-hand gypsum plaque, and the carbonised remains found during the excavation indicate that this is where the wooden seat was supported. The area was screened off by gypsum partitions on either side. The drainage system can be seen very clearly from the door. All the water from the light wells, and the bathrooms and toilets ultimately found its way into the central drain which flowed into the river Kairatos.

Remains of precious objects were found in the small room with the wooden door, on the right, at the beginning of the corridor **(Treasury) 41.** As we proceed along this half-lit corridor, we can make out the lower part of a small stone staircase and its "sotto scala": here was found a group of miniature figurines in ivory and gold, belonging to a group of bull-fighting.

Continuing along the same corridor we come back to the ground floor level of the great staircase, at the point from which we started — an indication of the labyrinthine nature of the palace. We now proceed to cross the corridor in front of the Hall of the double axes, and come to the workshops area. On the walls to the right and

Types of Minoan Houses (Faience)

left we can see the sockets for the vertical and horizontal beams that were put here to resist earthquake shocks. The traces of the fire here are quite clear.

A little further on we can see the **Lapidary's Workshop 42.** Here basalt was worked; this is a greenish or reddish stone with yellow crystals that was imported from the area of Taygetos in the Peloponnese. The work on some of the stones was left half-finished: sawn and polished, they remained in their original position because of the sudden nature of the destruction.

Immediately after that we come to a small room known as the **Potter's Workshop 43,** and beyond this to the **Court of the Stone Spout 44,** from which a long stone conduit drained off the rain water into a blind well, today covered with an iron grille.

Opposite are the **Magazines of the Giant Pithoi 45.** These jars are the largest so far discovered, and date from the Protopalatial period.

Descending the staircase in front of us, which was restored by Evans, we now come to the **East Bastion 46** of **East Entrance C.** According to Evans, the area in which the bull-leaping took place lay beyond this point. Here we can see yet another sort of the drainage system. The rain water was conducted down a steep incline from the upper levels to the ground floor. The water would have picked up great speed as it flowed, however, and would have spilled out of the channel at the bends; to prevent this, an exceedingly clever system was adopted: the channel at the side of the staircase followed a parabolic curve, which checks the speed of the water so that its impetus is not so great when it gets to the corners. On the landings of the staircase there are two stone troughs to filter the water.

Returning in front of the Magazines of the Giant Pithoi, and continuing our ascent up the same staircase, we come to the **Corridor of the Draught Board 47,** which took its name from the royal gaming board (for playing) found here. It is made of ivory, rock crystal, gold, lapis lazuli and faience. The pawns were conical in shape and made of ivory. The whole is on exhibition in room IV of Heraklion Museum (case 57).

Near the point where the gaming board was found we can see the system that supplied drinking water, beneath an iron grille. The clay pipes have a ring fitting, and consist of cylinders tapered towards one end, so as to produce a greater head of water; this prevents the system from blocking up by washing away the various salts and not allowing them to adhere to the inside of the pipes.

Drinking water came from Mount Jouktas to the South of the palace. There are thus three different water and drainage systems in the palace: one for drinking water, one for rainwater and a third to carry away the sewage.

To the west can be seen the **Magazine of the Pithoi with the Medallions 48** with rosettes enclosed within the medallions in relief. We now proceed to the **North Entrance D.** This is the only part of the palace that has a controlling defence system. Fortifications are unknown in Minoan architecture, on account of the **Pax Minoica.** The passage was originally wider, but was later narrowed, probably to achieve securer defence. **The west 49** of the two bastions that controlled the entrance has been restored, and a copy of the fresco depicting the hunting of a wild bull has been placed here. There is an olive tree in low relief next to the animal, which is weary and panting as a result of the chase. The way in which these animals were caught is known from the scenes on the two gold cups found in the tomb at Vaphio near Sparta.

We descend to the northern entrance by the **Sloping Passage 50** below which runs the central drainage conduit. On the stone block at the side of it are incised mason's symbols, such as the trident, the double axe, and the star. The corridor ends to the North in a large room (the **"Custom House"** of Evans) **51,** with two columns and eight gypsum pillars.

To the left, and on a higher level is the **Northwest entrance 52** to the palace. Unlike the North entrance, which was the main one leading from the road coming from the harbour to the palace, this entrance probably had a religious character since it is flanked by a **Lustral basin 53.** There the visitor to the sanctuary, or anyone who was about to take part in the religious ceremonies, had to undergo lustration.

Proceeding to the West we come to the **Theatre 54,** an area which was connected with religious ritual, as can be seen from the miniature frescoes in the palace. It is believed that the royal box was on the raised podium, at the point where the tiers of seats meet, while the spectators sat on the steps of the tiers."The Theatral area" was in the middle.

Two paved causeways (one to the South crossing the seats, and one in the centre) meet just below at the **"Royal Road" 55** — the oldest in Europe, dating from the period of the first palace. The paving is in a relatively good state of preservation, as are the gutters for rain-water on either side. There were a variety of buildings on both sides of this road, such as the **"House of the Frescoes" 56** and the **"Armoury".** The Royal Road leads to the **Little palace,** on the other side of the modern road from Knossos to Heraklion.

In concluding our tour, we should note that only a few houses of the city around the palace have been excavated, and most of these were the residences of noble, wealthy Minoans.

Very close to the palace, on the south east side, are the remains of the **"House of the Chancel Screen" 57,** the **"SE House" 58,** the **"House of the Sacrificed Oxen"59,** the **"House of the Fallen Blocks"**

60, and the **"House of the Monolithic Pillars"**. It is worth visiting the Minoan Inn **(Caravanserai)** to the South, and the **"Southern Royal Tomb"** to the South of that and on the right of the road from Knossos to Spilia; this is a two-storied building with a burial chamber and a pillar crypt; also worth visiting is the **"Royal Villa"** to the NE of the palace and the **"Little Palace"**. To the West of the Little Palace is the **"Villa Ariadne"**, built by Evans in 1907 and used as a residence and for study purposes by himself and his colleagues.

The city's cemeteries stretched in almost every direction (on the sites of Sopata, Ayios Ioannis, Zafer-Papoura, Sanatorio, Gypsades, Monastiriako Kefali and Profitis Ilias), and the tombs in them have yielded many rich and valuable finds.

The visitor should bear in mind that to tour the Palace fully requires approximately two hours.

The Archaeological Museum of Heraklion

THE HERAKLION ARCHAEOLOGICAL

MUSEUM

The Museum was founded in 1883 by the "Philekpaideutikos Syllogos" ("Society of the Friends of Education"), under the presidency of Joseph Chatzidakis. Initially, when it was still simply a collection of antiquities, it was housed in two rooms near Ayios Minas. This space, however, soon proved to be too restricted to hold the precious objects that daily grew in number, especially after the proclamation of the independence of Crete in 1898. The collection therefore had to be moved to a large sector of the old Turkish barracks. At the same time attempts began to be made to build a proper Museum and to find a suitable plot of land for the purpose. Eventually, preference was given to the area formerly occupied by the monastery of Ay. Frangiskos. The building that was erected was demolished in 1937, however, since it was not proof against earthquakes, and its place was taken by the present Museum.

The rooms were opened to the public after the Second World War, with the material classified chronologically. The building has recently been extended.

The Museum houses ancient objects discovered at the most important archaeological sites in Crete: Knossos, Phaistos, Malia, Tylissos, Gortys, Ayia Triada, Mokhlos, Gournia, Zakros, in a great number of tombs, in the caves of Kamares, the Idaean cave, the Diktaean cave, the cave of Eileithyia, and so on.

The most interesting and best preserved of the finds are exhibited in the 20 rooms of the Museum. Minoan art is nowhere better represented, and this makes the Museum unique and has made it known the whole world over.

The visitor should be aware that about two hours are needed to see the Museum properly. To assist him, we refer only to the most important objects to be found in the showcases. The rooms have Latin numerals.

GROUND FLOOR

ROOM I

Neolithic (6000-2600 B.C.) and Minoan Prepalatial (2600-1900 B.C.) cultures.

Case 1

Pottery from the Neolithic period, found mainly in the neolithic settlement below the palace at Knossos, and in the cave of Eileithyia (top shelf). It is typified by hand made pottery, mainly of a broad shape, which was fired on an open hearth, and had a burnished surface with incised linear decoration.

Female steatopygous figurines, and votive animals. Stone maces, hammers, axes and bone tools.

Case 3

Pottery from the beginning of the Prepalatial period, from the tombs at Pyrgos (near Anopolis), Kyparissi, Partira, and the cave of Eileithyia; "Pyrgos style" vases, in the shape of a communion calice, with decoration achieved by a special technique (using a burnisher) attempting to imitate models made of wood; vases in the Ayios Onoufrios style, decorated with brown or black geometric designs on light background; double or triple ritual cups ("kernoi") that were used to make offerings of fruit or liquids to the deity.

Case 6

Excellent vases of the "Vassiliki style" coming from the district of Vassiliki (Ierapetra), and other parts of East Crete. The decoration was the result of uneven firing, which produces red and black mottles.

Case 7

Uniquely beautiful stone vases in a great variety of shapes and materials (steatite, alabaster, polychrome marbles, limestone) discovered in tombs on the island of Mokhlos in East Crete. There are two particularly fine pyxis lids with handles in the shape of a resting dog; one was found at Zakro.

Case 8

Pottery typical of the end of the Prepalatial period, from Vassiliki and Mokhlos. The vases are decorated with white and red on a black background.

Model of a ship, sacred horns and a vase (rhyton) in the shape of a female figure (undoubtedly that of the mother goddess).

Case 10

Pottery from Palaikastro (Sitia), an important Minoan centre in East Crete. The vases with plastic decoration inside them are very interesting, especially the small bowl with a whole herd of animals and their herdman. The clay models of a four-wheeled chariot and a ship illustrate methods of transport at the end of the Prepalatial period.

Case 11

Particularly interesting sealstones from the prepalatial tombs at Messara, in a variety of shapes (some of them are plastic, in the shape of quadruped, birds, and so on) and in different materials, mainly ivory and steatite. In most cases they have one or two surfaces for producing sealings, but the sealstone from Phourni (Arkhanes) (no. 2260) has thirteen. Some sealstones came to Crete from Egypt or Asia, like the Babylonian cylinder seal (1098) from the period of King Hammurabi (1750 B.C.)

Case 13

Cycladic figurines of a naked female figure, from the tholos tombs in the Messara and from Teke (Heraklion); ivory figurines from the Messara and the cave at Trapeza (Lassithi). Razor blades of Melian obsidian (a volcanic material resembling a dark crystalline glass), and three small needle-cases of schist, which were also used as reels for winding the thread.

Case 14

An important collection of bronze weapons and tools. Bronze dagger blades found in the tholos tombs in the Messara and the cave at Trapeza. The short blades are the earliest. In most cases the handle has perished, since it was made of wood. The only handles to survive are of ivory or stone. The richest daggers are of silver. A variety of tools, tweezers, needles.

Case 17

Jewellery from the tholos tombs in the Messara and from Mokhlos. Gold diadems and bands for covering the eyes of the dead.

Necklaces of rock crystal, amethyst and carneol.

Small gold model of a frog, decorated in the granulation technique . Two gold female breasts, magic eyes, gold chains and rosettes. A very small gold pin-head in the shape of a human head.

ROOM II

Protopalatial Period.
Palaces at Knossos, Malia and Peak sanctuaries (1900-1700 B.C.).

Case 19

Pottery and stone vases from tombs and from the lower levels of the palace at Malia. Jug incised with a primitive representation of the fertility goddess, and a libation vase in the shape of a mother goddess. Stone moulds for making bronze double axes. Vessel with holes, used for squeezing fruit.

Case 20

Vases and "bell-shaped" figurines from Tylissos. The figurines may be imitations of horned masks worn by the priests during religious ceremonies. Small jugs and figurines from a sacred deposit at Gournes (Heraklion).

Case 23

Kamares-ware pottery from the palace at Knossos. The polychrome vases in this style took their name from the cave near the village of Kamares, in which they were first discovered. A number of the cups have a very thin wall and are therefore called "eggshell ware". Faience model of a ritual mask from Poros (Heraklion), with horns; the main features of the faces are rendered.

Case 24

Clay votive figurines of humans and animals from the peak sanctuaries at Petsophas (Palaikastro), Kalo Khorio (Pediada) and Jouktas (Arkhanes). The men are naked, save for a kilt and a dagger, and the women are wearing a broad skirt and a wide head-covering, and are depicted offering worship.

"Tri-Columnar Shrine" with doves, symbolizing the "epiphany" of the deity.

Model of a palanquin for the transportation of a priestess or goddess.

Case 25

The "Town Mosaic". It is made of fine plaques of faience, which may have once formed the incrustated decoration of a wooden box. They are representing two or three storied buildings with glass panels in the windows and attics on the flat roof. They also show scenes of hunting around them.

On the other side of the case there is a display of clay tablets, inscribed with a hieroglyphic script, from Knossos and Malia.

Case 29

Three large Kamares-ware vases from the palace at Knossos. The pithos with the palm-tree motif is particularly interesting.

ROOM III

Protopalatial Period.
The Palace at Phaistos (1900-1700 B.C.).

Case 34

A notable collection of Kamares-ware from the palace at Phaistos. These are amongst the finest in terms of shapes, designs and colour.

Cup with a stellar symbol in the shape of a swastika.

Case 41

The Phaistos disc. This was discovered in 1908, and is made of clay with 45 hieroglyphic characters separately impressed on both sides by means of punches, and arranged in a spiral running from the rim to the centre. It dates from the beginning of the Neopalatial period and the contents of the text are still unknown. Many attempts have been made to decipher it, but none has found general acceptance. It is possibly a religious hymn.

Case 42

Offering tables and other vessels connected with religion, from the palace at Phaistos. Tall fruitstand with a scene of a goddess raising her hands, while priestesses dance around her. A similar sacred dance is depicted on the inner surface of a bowl.

Case 43

Wonderful pottery, undoubtedly meant for a royal table. A stand for holding vases with dentelated rim ; krater with plastic flowers and small decorative lilies. Wine-jug, similarly decorated, from the same set.

ROOM IV

Neopalatial Period.
Palaces at Knossos - Phaistos - Malia (1700-1450 B.C.).

Case 45

Pottery from the palace at Knossos. The famous "Vases of the lilies". Cups with monochrome decoration in depicting of branches in the so-called floral style. "Epinetron" — an implement used while carding wool.

Case 46

Tubular vessels from Knossos for keeping the sacred snakes. The theory has been put forward that the cups attached to them held honey and milk to feed the snakes. They may have been offering vessels of the "kernos" type. Model of a wild honeycomb with a snake crawling over it. Vessel with holes, and snakes in relief, and small libation vases.

Case 47

Large bronze saw from the palace at Malia. Stone head of a royal sceptre, in the shape of an axe ending with the fore-part of a leopard opposite the cutting edge.

Case 50

Objects from the Temple Repositories in the palace at Knossos: faience figurines of the snake goddess and her daughter. A snake is crawling over the outstretched arms of the mother goddess, and stretching its head towards the top of her tiara. The daughter-goddess is holding two snakes and there is a little panther sitting on her head.

Coloured shells from the decoration of the altar, and plastic marine and vegeration motifs from the same area.

Case 51

Steatite rhyton in the shape of a bull's head — a masterpiece of Minoan sculpture from the Little palace at Knossos. The right side is original, the left restored. The eye is made of crystal, the mucoid of jasper, and the line round the muzzle of mother of pearl. It was hollow inside, with a hole in the nape; through this the rhyton was filled with the liquid (perhaps the blood of the sacrificial bull), which was poured out through another hole, in the muzzle, at the moment of the libation. The bull was the most sacred animal of Minoan religion and embodies the power of fertility.

Case 52

Ritual sword from the palace at Malia, with a gold-inlaid handle and a pommel of crystal, "insignium dignitatis" symbolizing the royal power. The smaller sword appears to have belonged to an acrobat from the palace, who used to set it upright and then leap over it (this explains the scene, on the foil covering the lower part of the pommel, of an acrobat bent in somersault as he jumps).

Fragments of stone vases with relief scenes of religious ritual, from Knossos. Also from Knossos is the small crystal plaque depicting an acrobat leaping over a bull. Another plaque, from Phaistos, has a scene of a procession of demons or priests wearing animal masks.

Case 55

Sacred objects found along with the snake goddesses. The marble cross was very probably a stellar or solar symbol. Fine faience plaques showing, in low relief, the mother goddess, in the form of a cow, and the daughter goddess, in the form of a wild goat suckling, or playing with her young.

Bronze trays from weighing scales and lead and stone weights.

Case 56

An ivory acrobat (bull leaper) from Knossos — an exceptional piece of craftsmanship with an admirable rendering of anatomical detail. He is portrayed executing the dangerous somersault over the back of the bull, and formed part of a larger group, the rest of which has not survived.

Case 57

Royal gaming board from the palace at Knossos, wrought entirely of precious materials (ivory, rock crystal, faience and lapis lazuli). The ivory pawns are reminiscent of the "pessoi" with which Homeric heroes amused themselves.

ROOM V.

Neopalatial Period: advanced and final phases.
The Palace at Knossos (1450-1380 B.C.).

Case 62

Large tall stone lamps from Knossos. They carry relief decoration, and there are two receptacles to hold the wick. A model standard weight with octopus in relief; it may have been used to check the weight of the bronze talents. They are all of red stone (porphyrite).Stone hair, possibly from a sphinx that has not survived. Objects imported from Egypt, such as the lid of an alabaster vessel inscribed with the name of the Pharaoh Chyan, and the figurine of a seated male figure, with the name of the official Uzer.

Case 66

Loaf-shaped"**alabastra**", possibly to hold perfumed oil. They were found in the Throne room of the palace at Knossos, and were apparently being used in some ritual when the palace suffered its final destruction.

Case 67

Three-handled "palace style" amphoras from Knossos, with marine decoration (octopuses, rocks, seaweed, etc.).

Case 69

The long side holds tablets and other objects inscribed with the Minoan Linear A Script, from important centres in Central and East Crete. They seem to be accounts of some kind, but have not yet been deciphered. Linear A, which can also be seen on offering tables and vases (short side), developed into Linear B during the Mycenaean phase of Cretan civilisation. This latter script is also found in Mainland Greece; it presents us with an earlier form of the Greek language, the Mycenaean dialect, and was deciphered by Ventris and Chadwick. Tablets in this script, dating from the final destruction of the palace at Knossos, are displayed on the other side of the case; they contain lists of men, animals, farm produce, weapons and other objects belonging to the palace.

Case 70A

Clay model of a Minoan house, from Arkhanes. The detail of it makes it unique as an example of Minoan architecture. The windows are shown, and also the entrance with its column, the light well, the hall with columns, the balcony, the staircase, and the pergola.

ROOM VI

Neopalatial and Postpalatial Periods.
Tombs from the areas around Knossos and Phaistos
(1380-1200 B.C.).

Case 71

Vases and plastic clay groups representing a sacred dance and the worship of the dead, from the tholos tomb at Kamilari, in the area of Ayia Triada.

Case 75A

Horse burial or sacrifice from a tholos tomb at Arkhanes.

Case 78

Helmet with boar's teeth sewn on leather, from a post-palatial tomb at Zafer Papoura (Knossos). It is the only one of its kind from Crete, though the type is known from excavations on the mainland. It is similar to the helmet of Meriones described by Homer.

Case 79A

Ivory pyxis with a relief scene representing the capture of a wild bull by armed men. It comes from a tomb at the harbour of Knossos, at what is today Katsambas.

Case 81

Small finds from the tombs at Knossos and Katsambas: mirror handle and comb with sphinxes in relief, a pyxis lid and a model of a ship, all of ivory. Necklaces of precious stones, gold diadems to adorn the foreheads of the dead, trays for scales to weigh the souls of the dead, pawns and "knuckle-bones", sealstones and a scarab of the Pharaoh Amenophis III.

Case 82

Clay and stone vases from the tombs of Katsambas. Egyptian amphora of alabaster with an inscription of Tuthmoses III - a gift to the court at Knossos. Chaffing pans that still contain coals for burning aromatic substances inside the tomb.

Case 84

A variety of weapons from the tombs of Zafer Papoura and Sanatorio in the region of Knossos: swords (some of them with gold handles) daggers, spears, knives, arrows.

Case 85

Bronze helmet with cheek-pieces and a hole to fix the crest; from a tomb in the area of Sanatorio (Knossos).

Case 86

Necklaces with beads in a variety of shapes, made of glass paste, gold, carneol, amethyst, faience, steatite, etc.; from the royal tombs of Phaistos at Kalyvia, and from the tholos tomb at Kamilari (Ayia Triada).

Case 87

Very fine jewellery from a number of different tombs in Central and East Crete. Royal gold ring, with a scene of a goddess descending from heaven, while priestesses with raised arms invoke her (the "epiphany" of a deity). From the tomb at Isopata (Knossos).

Necklaces with beads of different shapes, from the tombs of Knossos and Phaistos. Gold mask, which covered the face of the dead, from Mouliana (Sitia).

Case 88

Objects from the tombs at Arkhanes: necklaces with beads of gold and semi-precious stones, an excellent gold ring with a religious scene, fragments of the ivory decoration from a wooden pyxis (jewellery box), small plaques of ivory representing scenes of warriors or animals, a bronze mirror with an ivory handle, decorated with a relief scene of a suckling cow.

ROOM VII

Neopalatial period.
Villas and caves of Central Crete
(1700-1450 B.C.).

To the right of the entrance there are three very large sacred bronze double axes from the Megaron of Nirou. The bases and hafts have been restored in accordance with the axes pictured on the Ayia Triada sarcophagus. The Minoan name for the double axe is "labrys", from which the word Labyrinth is derived. Stone double horns are exhibited near the axes; these are also symbols of Minoan religion, and come from the same megaron.

Case 92

Groups of bronze figurines of worshippers, votive animals, bronze knives, small double axes, a small waggon pulled by oxen, a stone offering table, from the Diktaean cave and the caves at Skotino (Pediada) and Patsos (Rethymno).

Case 93

Pottery from the villa at Ayia Triada in the Messara. Pitcher with double axes combined with sacred knots. Carbonised remains of food: beans, barley, dried figs, etc.

Case 94

The rhyton of the harvesters and winnowers, of black steatite (only the upper part is preserved). It comes from the villa at Ayia Triada, and is one of the most important exhibits in the Museum. It is adorned with a relief showing a procession of men returning from harvesting and winnowing, carrying their tools on their shoulders. A group of musicians is singing hymns of thanksgiving to the deity, to the rhythm of a "seistrum" held by their leader.

Case 95

Also from Ayia Triada is the "Cup of the Report" or of the "officer", so called after the scene decorating it. An officer with a sword on his shoulder and a lustral sprinkler in his other hand, for the sacred purification, is standing to attention, as though he is making a report, before a king or a prince. The latter has carefully arranged hair, is holding a sceptre, and wears a necklace round his neck. The officer is followed by three others who are bearing the hides of large animals, which have either been sacrificed or caught during a hunt.

Case 96

Conical rhyton, again from Ayia Triada. It has four bands of relief decoration representing sacred athletic contests (jumping, boxing, wrestling and bull-leaping).

Case 99

"Talents", bronze units of a standard shape and weight (about 29 kilos), that served as a means of exchange. Some of them are incised with symbols in the Cretan or Cypriote script (showing that Cyprus exported bronze). They were discovered at Ayia Triada.

Case 101.

Gold objects and jewellery: miniature magic pendant with representations of an open palm, a snake, a snail, a scorpion and a spider, perhaps to ward off the dangerous serpents and insects; bulls-heads and small lions, from Ayia Triada. The famous piece of gold jewellery showing hornets or wasps, sucking a drop of honey from the honeycomb, a gold pin with a flower at the end of it, gold leaves and earrings, from the cemetery of Chryssolakkos near Malia. Gold votive double axes from the cave at Arkalokhori. Gold rings with religious scenes.

ROOM VIII

Neopalatial period.
The Palace at Zakros (1600-1450 B.C.).

On the west wall there is a relief spiral frieze, of stucco, which comes from the palace Banquet Hall.

Case 109

Excellent vase made of rock crystal. Around the neck there is a ring of pieces of rock crystal joined together with gilded ivory leaves. The handle consists of beads of crystal threaded on a gilded bronze wire, which is now of green colour as a result of oxidation.

Case 111

Rhyton made of chlorite, the surface of which was originally covered with gold leaf. The relief depicts a peak sanctuary with 4 wild goats sitting on the roof. The large door is decorated with spirals and there is an enclosure with altars of various types. At the side, two more "agrimis", rendered with amazing realism, are escalading over the rocky mountain, and hawks are hovering over sacred double horns.

Case 113

Two elephant's tusks, brought from Syria as the basic material for miniature art, bronze talents, marine style and floral style vases. Fine wine-jug with small argonauts.

Case 115

Bronze saws; two of them are folded for transport or storage and the third, which is of enormous size, has two handles (parts of one, only, survives). Double axes, the rim of a bronze disc decorated with double axes, square pieces of bronze sheet with papyrus flowers.

Case 116

Rhyton in the shape of a bull's head, similar to the one discovered at Knossos (case 51).

Case 118

A series of stone ritual vases from the sacred treasury. A wonderful amphora with a double mouth and skillfully worked handles, rhytons in the shape of small bull's heads, made of faience, hammers, communion calices.

ROOM IX

Neopalatial period.
East Crete (1700-1450 B.C.).

Case 119

Clay and stone vases from the settlement at Palaikastro (Sitia). Clay grill and funnel, clay rhyton in the shape of a bull's-head, bronze figurines and animals, stone lamps and offering tables.

Case 123

Clay figurines of men and women in an attitude of worship, and with a great variety of hairstyles: from the peak sanctuary at Piskokefalo (Sitia). Clay models of shrines crowned with sacred horns and of sacred insects of the specy "rhinoceros oryctes" which can still be found in Crete. Real insects from the area of sanctuary are displayed on the same shelf.

Case 127

Weapons and tools for everyday uses, from East Crete. Bronze double axes, swords, fish-hooks, picks, razor-blades etc.

Case 128

Choice sealstones of the Neopalatial period, representing animals, flowers, deities, mostly made of semi-precious stones; from Central and Eastern Crete.

ROOM X

Postpalatial period·
(1380-1100 B.C.)·

Case 132

Pottery from Palaikastro and Gournia. Small stirrup amphoras, small jugs, censers and a censer lid. The vases decorated with birds are particularly interesting. Clay representation of a circular dance, from Palaikastro. The dancers are holding each other's shoulders, and the musician is playing the lyra in the middle, just as in the modern Cretan dance "pentozalis".

Case 133

Large schematized clay figurines of female deities from Gazi (Heraklion). They have sacred symbols on their heads, such as horns, birds and poppy pistils.

Case 138

Double vases from the north entrance of the palace at Knossos. Figurines and animals from Phaistos. Small donkey carrying two amphoras. Goddess riding on a horse, from Arkhanes. Small clay chests.

Case 139

Stone moulds for making jewellery, double axes and sacred objects.

Case 143

Strange clay figurines and animals, a girl on a swing, a ship, from Ayia Triada.

Case 144

Bronze tools and weapons from the tombs at Mouliana, Episkopi and Stamious. The safety-pins (brooches) that begin to be used during this period are interesting, as indicating a change in the style of dress; the round bronze objects are attachments of shields (not cymbals, as was originally thought).

ROOM XI

Sub-Minoan and Protogeometric periods.
(1100-800 B.C.).

Case 146

Pottery from the geometric settlement at Vrokastro at the province of Ierapetra. Large cinerary urns decorated with scenes of mourning. Bronze tripod. Models of horses and anthropomorphic masks.

Case 148

Large clay figures of goddesses with raised hands, and with sacred symbols on the diadems crowning their heads. Rhyton in the shape of a curious chariot pulled by oxen. Only the heads of the animals have been rendered, attached to the chariot itself.

They come from the settlement of Karfi (Lassithi), which was founded after the conquest of Crete by the Dorians.

Case 149

Clay figurines and other dedications from the cave of Eileithyia at Inatos in South Crete. The figurines are connected with human fertility: loving couples, pregnant women, and women suckling their babies. The cult in the cave continued down to Roman times.

Case 153

Tools and weapons made of the new metal, iron, coming mainly from the geometric tombs at Fortetsa in the area of Knossos.
Iron brooches that were used to fasten the Doric peplos (cloak).

Case 155

Important early geometric vases, some of them with animal and human figures from Teke (Knossos).

ROOM XII

Mature Geometric and Orientalizing periods.
(800-650 B.C.).

Case 162

Proto-Corinthian aryballoi from the tombs of Fortetsa (Knossos). Sacred tree with birds, symbolizing the epiphany of the deity, on the branches. Models of monkeys and other animals. Small model of a boat with a passenger.

Case 163

Pottery in the "orientalizing style" from Arkades (Afrati), influenced by the art of the peoples of the East; it is decorated with sphinxes, lions, winged horses etc.
Two particularly distinctive pieces are the "cinerary urn" with a scene of the dead man and a woman mourning him, and the "wine-jug" depicting a loving couple, may be Theseus and Ariadne.

Case 164

Bronze votive belt from Fortetsa, with repoussé decoration. The scene is representing a chariot attack against a shrine with the holy Triad (one male and two female figures).

Case 170

Gold jewellery from a tomb at Teke (Knossos). Pendant of rock crystal in the shape of a crescent with chains on which hang the symbols of the moon and the sun. Gold band with a repeated scene of a god taming a lion.

On the east wall there are large 7th century pithoi, with relief and impressed decoration, from ancient Lyttos. There are similar pithoi from Arkades on the west wall.

ROOM XIII

Minoan sarcophagi.

The clay sarcophagi were widely used during the post-palace period. The dead were laid inside them in contracted position. They are of two types: those in the shape of a chest or box with four feet and a lid, and those in the shape of a bath. The motifs painted on them are decorative, or are taken from nature (schematized flowers, fishes octopuses) or have a religious significance (double axes, sacred horns etc.).

The ship depicted on one of the sarcophagi may symbolize the journey of the deceased to the other world.

FIRST FLOOR

ROOM XIV

Neopalatial period.
Frescoes
(1600-1380 B.C.).

The most distinctive of the frescoes on the north wall of the room from west to east, are:

The large "Procession Fresco" from the palace at Knossos. There were about 360 figures in the composition, but very little has survived, and only one head has been preserved – that of the "Cupbearer", near the door. The scene portrays young men holding vases in their hands and proceeding from two opposite directions to a point in the middle. Here was the queen, princess or priestess, the representative of the Great goddess.

A griffin amongst papyrus flowers. This decorated the "Throne room" of the palace at Knossos.

A charming scene of a wild cat prowling amongst thick vegetation and stalking a bird, which is sitting all unaware on a rock. From the Villa at Ayia Triada.

On the south wall, we may note the following frescoes (East to West):

— Large figure-of-eight shields made of bull's hides sewn together (the stitches can be seen). From the palace at Knossos.

— A relief fresco known as the "Prince with the Lilies" or the "Priest-King". He is wearing a crown of lilies and peacock's feathers. He may have been leading the sacred griffin, or a sphinx, with his left hand. The fresco was found at the end of the Corridor of the procession, in the palace at Knossos.

— Bull's head in low relief, from a scene that adorned the North entrance of the palace at Knossos.

— The "Ladies in Blue" fresco. The heads were restored with the help of other frescoes and very small fragments. From the east part of the palace at Knossos.

— The "Fresco of the dolphins" playing in the waves. From the Queen's Megaron in the palace at Knossos.

— The "Fresco with the partridges". From the Caravanserai, to the South of the palace at Knossos. There is a hoopoe amongst the partridges.

— The "Toreaoor fresco", or bull-fighting, from the east wing of the palace at Knossos. Both men and women took part in this sport (the men are rendered in a red colour, and the women in white). The fresco was representing different stages in the sport at successive panels. Athletes are grasping the bull by the horns, jumping on its back, and then landing upright on the ground behind its tail.

— The "Lily frescoes" from the Villa of the lilies at Amnissos. White lilies and red irises, either standing on altar, or arranged in stepped fashion.

Case 171

In the centre of the room is the unique stone s a r c o p h a g u s from Ayia Triada. On one of the long sides there is a scene of a bull-sacrifice in honour of the dead king. The bull has already been sacrificed,trussed on a table, while two other animals await their turn. A musician playing a double pipe is leading a procession of women. At the extreme right a priestess is making offerings of libations and fruit before the precinct of the sacred tree, which is crowned with horns.

On the other side opposite, a priestess or a queen with a crown, who may perhaps be the widow of the dead man, is carrying buckets full of the sacrificial blood, to give to another priestess in front of her; the latter is emptying them between two double axes with birds on top of them. They are followed by a musician playing a seven-string lyra. Three priests are walking in the opposite direction to this procession. They are holding models of animals and a ship in their hands, which they are about to offer to the dead man, who can be seen in front of the entrance to the tomb, behind an altar. Both of the short sides of the sarcophagus have a picture of a chariot and two women; on one side the chariot is drawn by horses, and on the other by griffins.

ROOM XV

Neopalatial period
(1600-1380 B.C.).

Note the following frescoes on the west wall:
— Priestesses dancing in the sacred grove (of olives) at Knossos. The ritual is being keenly watched by a crowd of men and women.

— Festival before the "Tripartite shrine" in the palace at Knossos. Women of the court are standing or sitting to the right and left of the shrine. Here, too, the ritual is being followed by a large number of men, and a few women.

— The fresco of the "Parisienne", as it was named by Evans' workmen as soon as it was discovered in the palace at Knossos. The sacred knot on her shoulder shows that she is a priestess or a deity.

ROOM XVI

Neopalatial period.
Frescoes.
(1600-1380 B.C.).

The outstanding fresco on the west wall is that of the "Saffron gatherer". It was found on the NW "insula" of the palace at Knossos and depicts a blue monkey gathering saffron. Evans thought that the gatherer was a human being (his restoration is exhibited next to the original).

— There are three compositions from the "House of the Frescoes" at Knossos:

— A "Blue bird" in a rocky landscape.
— "Blue Monkey" in a similar background.
— Monkeys amongst saffron and papyrus plants.

ROOM XVII

Yamalakis Collection

Styl. Yamalakis, a doctor from Heraklion, built up a very distinguished collection through personal purchases, which he sold to the Greek State in 1962. It consists of objects from all periods, ranging from the Neolithic to the period of the Turkish occupation. They are mainly from Central and Eastern Crete.

ROOM XVIII

Miniature art from the Archaic, Classical, Hellenistic, and Greco-Roman periods. (7th century B.C. - 4th century A.D.)

Clay and bronze figurines, animals, vases, Bronze weapons, jewellery, and coins from the above periods.

GROUND FLOOR

ROOM XIX

Monumental art of the archaic period.
(7th and 6th centuries B.C.).

It is mainly sculpture of the archaic period that is on display here. Amongst the sculptures we may note the large frieze from the temple on the acropolis of Prinias (perhaps the ancient Rhizenia), with a parade of horses in relief, and the seated goddesses from the interior portal of the same temple.

The three hammered bronze statues from the temple of Apollo at Dreros (the "Delphinion") are also of importance; they probably represent Apollo, Artemis and Leto (case 210).

In cases 208 and 209 are displayed the famous votive shields from the Idaean cave, with scenes in relief upon them.

Stele of blackish stone, with the Curetic hymn to Cretan Zeus. From the sanctuary of Diktaean Zeus at Palaikastro.

ROOM XX

Greek and Roman sculpture.
(5th century B.C. - 4th century A.D.).

There is little sculpture from the classical period in Crete, because the unending civil strifes between the cities on the island hold against the development of art, and contributed to the isolation of the island from the rest of Greece. There is an interesting metope from a 4th century temple at Knossos, representing Herakles bringing Cerberus from Hades, and a fine classical funerary relief of a hunter from Achlada. Works from the Roman period are much more numerous, for the island then recovered its internal peace and prosperity. Most of them are from Gortys, Knossos, Lyttos, Chersonessos and Ierapetra. The best of them are copies of classical works.

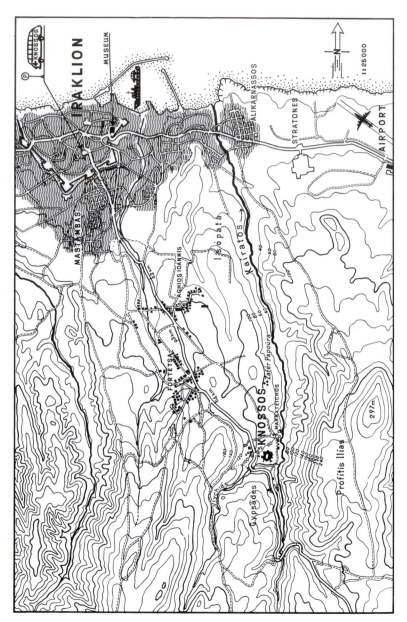

Μουσείο Ηρακλείου: Ο "πρίγκηπας με τα κρίνα". Τοιχογραφία από την Κνωσό.
Heraklion Museum: "The Prince with Lilies". Fresco from Knossos.
Musée d' Héraclion: "Le Prince aux fleurs de lis". Fresque du palais de Cnossos.
Museum von Heraklion: "Der Prinz mit den Lilien". Wandgemalde von Knossos.
Museo di Eraclion: "Il Principe dai fiori di giglio". Affresco del palazzo di Cnosso.

Κνωσός: Κεντρικό κλιμακοστάσιο Δ. πτέρυγας του ανακτόρου.
Knossos: Staircase to the west wing of the palace.
Cnossos: L' escalier de l' aile ouest du palais.
Knossos: Treppenhaus der Westflügel der Palastes.
Cnosso: Grande scalinata dell' ala occidentale.

Κνωσός: Οι Δυτικές αποθήκες.
Knossos: West magazines.
Cnossos: Les magasins occidentaux.
Knossos: Die Westmagazine.
Cnosso: Magazzini occidentali.

Κνωσός: Τα "Νότια προπύλαια".
Knossos: South Propylaeum.
Cnossos: Les Propylées Sud.
Knossos: Süd Propyläen.
Cnosso: Propilei meridionali.

Κνωσός: Η Βόρεια είσοδος.   Knossos: Nordeingang.
Knossos: North Entrance.   Cnosso: Entrata settentrionale.
Cnossos: L' entrée Nord.

Κνωσός: Το "Μέγαρο της βασίλισσας"
Knossos: Queen's Megaron.
Cnossos: Megaron de la Reine.

Knossos: Megaron der Königin.
Cnosso: Megaron della regina.

Κνωσός: Ο "Θρόνος του Μίνωα".   Knossos: Der Thron von Minos.
Knossos: The Throne of Minos.   Cnosso: Il Trono di Minos.
Cnossos: Le Thrône de Minos.

Κνωσός: Το "Μεγάλο κλιμακοστάσιο". Βεράντα με Τοιχογραφία ασπίδων.
Knossos: The great Staircase. The Hall with the Shield fresco.
Cnossos: Le grand escalier. La Veranda aux boucliers.

Knossos: Grosse Treppe. Di Veranda mit den Schilden.
Cnosso: La grande scalinata: Una veranda a colonne e l' affresco degli scudi.

Μουσείο Ηρακλείου: Η "Παριζιάνα". Τοιχογραφία από την Κνωσό.
Heraklion Museum: The "Parisienne". Fresco from Knossos.
Musée d' Héraclion: La "Parisienne". La fresque du Palais de Cnossos.
Museum von Heraklion: Die "Pariserin". Wandgemälde von Knossos.
Museo di Eraclion: La "Parigina". Affresco del palazzo di Cnosso.

Μουσείο Ηρακλείου: Τα "Ταυροκαθάψια". Τοιχογραφία από την Κνωσό.
Museum von Heraklion: Das "Stierspringen". Wandgemälde von Knossos.
Heraklion Museum: "The Bull-fight". Fresco from Knossos.
Museo di Eraclion: Affresco della "giostra" col toro selvatico". Palazzo di Cnosso.
Musée d' Héraclion: Fresque de la "Tauromachie". Palais de Cnossos.

Μουσείο Ηρακλείου: Οι "Γαλάζιες κυρίες". Τοιχογραφία από την Κνωσό.
Heraklion Museum: "The Blue Ladies". Fresco from the Palace of Knossos.
Musée d' Héraclion: La fresque des "Dames en bleu". Palais de Cnossos.

Museum von Heraklion: Die "Damen im Blau". Wandgemälde von Knossos.
Museo di Eraclion: Affresco delle "Signore azzurre". Palazzo di Cnosso.

Μουσείο Ηρακλείου: Ο "Δίσκος της Φαιστού".
Heraklion Museum: The Disc of Phaestos.
Musée d' Héraclion: La Disque de Phaistos.
Museum von Heraklion: Der Diskus von Phaistos.
Museo di Eraclion: Il Disco di Festós.

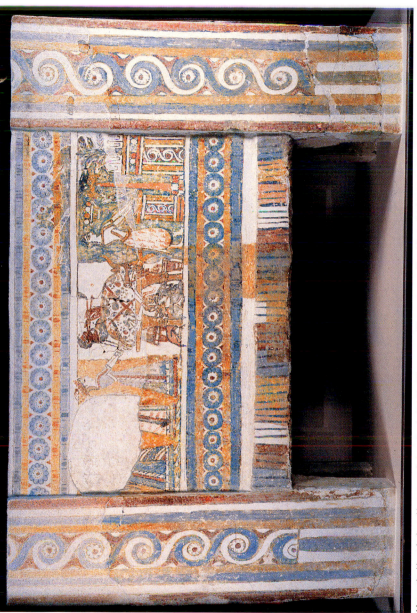

Μουσείο Ηρακλείου: Χρυσό κόσμημα, από το Χρυσόλακκο Μαλίων.
Heraklion Museum: Gold jewel Chrysolakkos of Malia.
Musée d' Héraclion: Bijou d' or provenant de Malia.

Museum von Heraklion: Goldschmuck hervorragender Handwerkskunst aus Malia.
Museo di Eraclion: Gioiello d' oro finemente lavorato proveniente da Malia.

Μουσείο Ηρακλείου: Οι "Θεές των φιδιών" από την Κνωσσό.   Museum von Heraklion: "Göttinnen der Schlangen" von Knossos.
Heraklion Museum: "Snake goddesses" from Knossos.   Museo di Eraclion: Dee dai serpenti. Palazzo di Cnosso.
Musée d' Héraclion: "Déesses aux serpents", de Cnossos.

Μουσείο Ηρακλείου: Ρυτό από στεατίτη σε μορφή κεφαλής ταύρου. Μικρό ανάκτορο Κνωσού.
Heraklion Museum: Libation vase (rhyton) in the form of a bull-head. Found in the Little Palace of Knossos.
Musée d' Héraclion: Vase à libation en forme de tête de taureau. Petit palais de Cnossos.
Museum von Heraklion: Spendegefäss in der Form eines Stierkopfes. Kleiner Palast von Knossos.
Museo di Eraclion: Vaso per libazioni (rhyton) a forma di testa taurina, in steatite.